Vietnam

by Sarah E. De Capua

Content Adviser: Thong Nguyen,
Second Secretary for Press, Information, and Cultural Affairs,
Embassy of the Socialist Republic of Vietnam
in the United States of America

Reading Adviser: Dr. Linda D. Labbo,
Department of Reading Education, College of Education,
The University of Georgia

 COMPASS POINT BOOKS

Minneapolis, Minnesota

FIRST REPORTS

Compass Point Books
3109 West 50th Street, #115
Minneapolis, MN 55410

Visit Compass Point Books on the Internet at *www.compasspointbooks.com*
or e-mail your request to *custserv@compasspointbooks.com*

Cover: Rowboats and town on Mekong River in Vietnam

Photographs©: Michael S. Yamashita/Corbis, cover, 10; Steve Raymer/Corbis, 4, 22, 23, 24, 25, 26; John
Elk III, 9, 21, 38, 39, 42–43; Brian A. Vikander/Corbis, 6, 11; PhotoDisc, 7; Photo Network/Sherman, 8,
18, 20; Giraudon/Art Resource, N.Y., 12; The Pierpont Morgan Library/Art Resource, N.Y., 13; Hulton/
Archive by Getty Images, 14–15, 16–17; Stephanie Maze/Corbis, 19; Chris Lisle/Corbis, 27, 40; Dean
Conger/Corbis, 28; Tim Page/Corbis, 29; Owen Franken/Corbis, 30, 35, 41; Jeff Greenberg/Visuals
Unlimited, 31; Wolfgan Kaehler/Corbis, 32–33; Leonard de Selva/Corbis, 34; Photo Network/Mitch Carter,
36–37; Ron Wise, 45 (bottom).

Editors: E. Russell Primm, Emily J. Dolbear, and Patricia Stockland
Photo Researcher: Svetlana Zhurkina
Photo Selector: Linda S. Koutris
Designer/Page Production: Bradfordesign, Inc./Biner Design
Cartographer: XNR Productions, Inc.

Library of Congress Cataloging-in-Publication Data
De Capua, Sarah.
  Vietnam / by Sarah De Capua.
    v. cm.— (First reports)
  Includes bibliographical references and index.
  Contents: An S-shaped country—Land and climate—History of Vietnam—Made in Vietnam—Life in
Vietnam—Festivals and holidays—Arts and literature—Vietnamese food and drink—Vietnamese
clothing—Vietnam today.
  ISBN 0-7565-0427-9 (hardcover)
  1. Vietnam—Juvenile literature. [1.Vietnam.] I. Title. II. Series.
  DS556.3 .D4 2003
  959.7—dc21   2002009930

Table of Contents

NOTE: In this book, words that are defined in the glossary are in **bold** the first time they appear in the text.

"Xin Cháo!"

"Xin cháo!" If you were visiting Vietnam, this is how you would greet someone.

Vietnam is a land of elephants, rhinoceroses, and tigers. Crocodiles, snakes, and many kinds of birds also live there. Many other things make Vietnam an interesting country.

▲ *Young men riding elephants in the Central Highlands in Ban Don, Vietnam*

▲ Map of Vietnam

Vietnam is a long, narrow country shaped like
a giant S. It is located in Southeast Asia. Vietnam is
1,030 miles (1,657 kilometers) long. Its narrowest
point is only 31 miles (50 kilometers) wide.

Vietnam touches three countries. China is north of Vietnam. Laos and Cambodia are west of Vietnam. Vietnam is bordered on two sides by water. The Gulf of Thailand touches the southwestern side. On the east side, the Gulf of Tonkin flows into the South China Sea.

▲ *The Gulf of Tonkin*

▲ *City Hall in Ho Chi Minh City*

Hanoi is the capital of Vietnam. This is where the country's central government is located. The largest city in Vietnam is Ho Chi Minh City. Other major cities include Haiphong, Da Nang, and Hue.

Land and Weather

▲ *Farm fields in the Central Highlands of Dalat, Vietnam*

Many different kinds of land make up Vietnam. The north is covered by the Hoang Lien Mountains. Vietnam's highest point is there—a mountain called Phan Si Pan, which is 10,312 feet (3,145 meters) high.

The central region is made up of the Truong Son Mountains. The Central Highlands lie south of these mountains. Flat land lies between the mountains and the coast of the South China Sea.

Two major Asian rivers flow through Vietnam. The Red River is in northern Vietnam. The Mekong River is in southern Vietnam. The **deltas** around these rivers make the land good for farming. Most of Vietnam's food is grown there. Most people live around the deltas and farm the land.

▲ *A nursery farm in the Mekong River delta*

Northern and southern Vietnam have different kinds of weather. In the north, there are two seasons. Winter is dry and cool. Summer is hot and wet. In the south, it is hot and wet all year long. The weather is cooler in the mountains, where there is more rain.

Monsoons bring a lot of rain to Vietnam. The monsoons occur from March to November. Between May and January, **typhoons** strike Vietnam. They cause floods that destroy crops and homes.

▲ *This hut was flooded during monsoon season.*

History of Vietnam

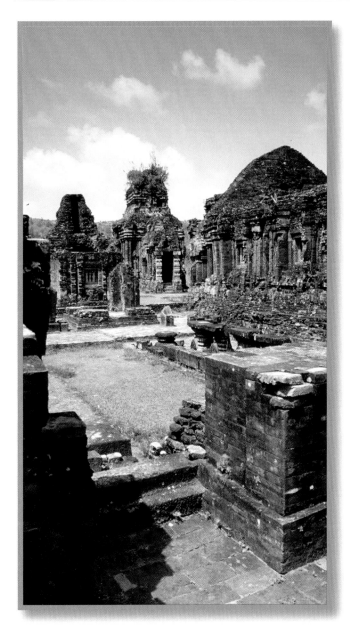

About 4,000 years ago, the **ancestors** of the Vietnamese lived in the Red River delta. Later, they moved south to find farmland. At the same time, the people of the Cham kingdom lived in the center of what is now Vietnam. The people of the Khmer kingdom lived in the south.

◀ *The ruins of an ancient Cham temple in central Vietnam*

This statue of a Dong-son warrior dates back to 400 B.C.

By 800 B.C., the Dong-son people lived in the Red River delta. They built ditches and canals there to control the river. They used the South China Sea to water their rice fields.

Around 250 B.C., the Dong-son people became part of a kingdom called Au Lac. Most of the people in the kingdom were rice farmers.

The Chinese arrived in 207 B.C. They took over the Red River delta. Two sisters named Trung Trac and Trung Nhi led others in a fight against the Chinese in A.D. 39. They succeeded in driving them out. In A.D. 42, the Chinese took over again.

China then ruled for nearly 900 years. During that time, the Vietnamese people often tried to regain their independence. They were finally successful and declared their independence from China in the year 939.

Starting in the 1400s, European explorers traveled to the country. The Portuguese arrived in 1516. The Dutch, British,

◄ *Portuguese ships arrived in Vietnam in the early sixteenth century.*

and French followed. By the 1880s, France controlled Vietnam.

On September 2, 1945, Vietnam announced its independence from France. It was then known as the Democratic Republic of Vietnam. In his speech, President Ho Chi Minh even quoted from the Declaration of Independence of the United States of America.

In 1946, a war between France and Vietnam started. The French gave up in 1954. That year, representatives from several countries met in Geneva, Switzerland. They decided to split the country briefly into two nations—North Vietnam and South Vietnam.

▲ *French soldiers using parachutes to invade Vietnam*

The two new nations struggled with one another. Fighting began again in 1957 and lasted until 1975. Soldiers in the north were supported by **communist** countries, including China and the Soviet Union. In 1965, the United States sent troops to fight against the North Vietnamese in the Vietnam War.

In the end, however, the U.S. effort failed. In 1973, the last U.S. troops left Vietnam. More than one million Vietnamese and more than 50,000 Americans died during the war.

The communists won the Vietnam War in 1975. The next year, the communists made North Vietnam and South Vietnam one country. It is now known as the Socialist Republic of Vietnam.

The National Assembly is the highest branch of government. Vietnam's assembly elects the president and vice president. It also approves the choice of prime minister and other cabinet members.

The Communist Party is the official political party of Vietnam. A group called the Politburo leads the country's Communist Party.

◀ *South Vietnamese troops preparing to board helicopters in 1966*

Made in Vietnam

▲ *Sheets of drying rice noodles*

Vietnam is one of the poorest countries in the world.
However, Vietnam does sell a number of its goods to
other countries.

Vietnam is one of the world's major sellers of rice.
It is grown throughout the country. Vietnam also
sells coffee, latex from rubber trees, and seafood to

other countries. Flowers called orchids are shipped all over the world. Vietnam ships coal, oil, and natural gas, too.

Small factories in Vietnam make farm tools, bicycles, and glass. Large factories process steel or food. Clothing is also made in large factories.

▲ Workers in a silk factory in Bao Lac

Life in Vietnam

Vietnamese people have a great love for their families. In most homes, grandparents, parents, and children all live together. Young people live with their parents until they marry.

△ *In Vietnam, several generations of a family often live together.*

▲ *A home made of bamboo and straw in the Mekong River valley*

Most Vietnamese live in the countryside. Their houses are made of brick with tile roofs. Some houses are made of wood or bamboo with roofs of palm leaves or straw. Recently, electricity has been made available to many communities far from the cities.

In cities, most Vietnamese live in apartment buildings with running water and electricity. Apartments usually have two or three rooms.

All Vietnamese children between the ages of five and eleven must go to school. They learn reading, writing, and mathematics.

After age eleven, good students may go on to four more years of school. They learn history, geography, literature, science, and another language. These students can choose to study English, Russian, or French.

▲ *Many Vietnamese students choose to study English as a second language.*

Most choose English. Other students go to schools to learn a trade such as carpentry or farming.

The school year begins in September and ends in May. Vietnamese children attend school six days a week, including Saturdays. Some children attend school from 7 A.M. to 11:15 A.M. Others attend school from 1 P.M. to 5 P.M. Students walk or ride bicycles to school. There are no school buses in Vietnam.

▲ *Students at a ceremony on their first day of class in September*

▲ *After school, some Vietnamese children relax and play games.*

After school, younger students often swim, jump rope, or play games. They play kickball, marbles, and hide-and-seek. Many students enjoy martial arts such as kung fu and karate. Older students play on soccer, track, volleyball, and tennis teams.

To relax in the evening, young people in cities gather in ice-cream shops or in their neighborhoods. Some take music or language lessons. Others go to the movies or cafés.

In the countryside, people relax by playing games. These include chess or cards. Many enjoy playing musical instruments. Few villagers own televisions, but they can gather in village cafés to watch videos.

Families in Vietnam like to relax together. They enjoy the beaches along the South China Sea. Ha Long Bay is a very popular vacation spot. The United Nations Educational, Scientific and Cultural Organization (UNESCO) calls Ha Long Bay one of

▲ *Children enjoying a day at the beach along the South China Sea*

the natural wonders of the world! It has more than 3,000 islands surrounded by crystal-clear water. The mountains near the city of Da Lat in the south are another popular vacation spot.

Badminton is a popular sport in Vietnam.

People of all ages enjoy an exercise called *thai cuc quyen*. It is a kind of slow-motion boxing related to Chinese kung fu. They do these exercises in public parks at sunrise.

In large cities, the government supports sports teams. Soccer teams are the most popular. The Vietnamese also enjoy swimming, tennis, volleyball, and badminton.

Festivals and Holidays

▲ *Lights and a colorful dragon float are part of this Tet celebration.*

The most important holiday in Vietnam is Tet. It celebrates the **lunar** New Year, which falls between late January and mid-February. The Vietnamese believe that the spirits of their ancestors return to Earth on Tet. People dress up, visit friends, take part in dragon parades, and eat large meals and special treats.

Another festival celebrated in Vietnam is Dong Nhan. This festival in March honors the Trung sisters. They are the women who led the fight against the Chinese in A.D. 39. In each village, two girls dress up as the sisters and ride an elephant during a parade.

Tet Trung Thu is a moon festival in mid-September to celebrate the crops. The festival is held at night when the moon is full. Children march in a parade. They carry colorful lanterns made of rice paper and bamboo. The lanterns are shaped like fish, toads, dragons, or stars.

△ *A fish-shaped lantern like this might be carried by a Vietnamese child in a Tet Trung Thu parade.*

The birthdays of new babies are important celebrations in Vietnam. Families celebrate the first birthday when a baby is one month old. They celebrate the second birthday when the baby is one year old. Family members bring the baby toys, clothing, and money. After age one, everyone celebrates his or her birthday on Tet.

Vietnam celebrates many government holidays. Two of them are Liberation Day on April 30 and National Day on September 2.

▲ *A National Day celebration in Hanoi*

Arts and Literature

▲ *A carved dragon on a wood temple column*

Vietnamese artists are famous for their jewelry, silk paintings, and wood carvings. Many of the finest silk paintings hang in temples and museums.

Folk songs, classical music, and choral music are all a part of Vietnamese music. Folk music includes children's songs, work songs, and festival songs. Musical instruments include bamboo flutes, skin drums, gongs, and cymbals.

▲ Cham tribe women from central Vietnam in traditional dress
for a performance in Ho Chi Minh City

Theater is called *hat tuong* in the north. It is known as *hat boi* in the south. It is based on Chinese opera.

Water puppetry began in Vietnam. Puppet shows are called *roi can* and are performed by people standing in the water. The people are hidden behind bamboo screens. The puppets act out well-known Vietnamese stories. The audience watches from the shore.

◀ *Roi can performances are popular entertainment in Vietnam.*

△ *Sculptures of animals from Vietnamese legend are often found in pagodas.*

Architecture is the art of designing and building structures. Much of Vietnam's architecture reflects the Chinese and French styles of building. Interesting sculptures can be found in temples, **pagodas,** and tombs. Figures of dragons decorate temples. Animals from legends can be seen in pagodas.

Vietnamese literature includes poetry and novels. The oldest poems are more than 1,000 years old. Nguyen Trai wrote poetry in the 1400s. Doan Thi Diem was a famous Vietnamese woman writer in the 1700s. Nguyen Du wrote Vietnam's best-loved novel in the 1800s. Modern-day writers include Ngo Tat To and Bao Ninh.

Vietnamese Food and Drink

▲ *A woman prepares soup at her street stand in Ho Chi Minh City.*

Vietnamese food differs from region to region. Vietnamese cooks use many fresh fruits, vegetables, and herbs. They cook mostly by steaming and boiling. Food can be hot and spicy.

Throughout Vietnam, rice is a part of every meal. People eat rice served plain or some-times sweetened with coconut. Rice is mixed into soups or fried with vegetables or meat.

The Vietnamese eat fish, shrimp, crab, pork, and duck. They do not eat a lot of beef.

An important ingredient in Vietnamese cooking is fish sauce. It is a mixture of fish juice, lime juice,

chopped peppers, garlic, and sugar. It is poured over rice or used as a dipping sauce for meat.

The Vietnamese do not usually end meals with fancy desserts. They are more likely to have fresh fruit.

Vietnamese enjoy a drink called *soda chanh*. This is crushed ice, lemon juice, and sugar mixed with soda water. It is especially delicious during hot weather. Coconut water and sugarcane juice are two other popular drinks. Green tea is often served with meals. A kind of thick, dark coffee is common at cafés.

◀ *Seafood is a common part of Vietnamese meals.*

Vietnamese Clothing

People prefer to wear loose, cotton clothing because of Vietnam's warm weather. Men and women often wear Western-style clothing. Men wear short-sleeved shirts and pants. Women wear pantsuits, pants and blouses, or long, loose dresses. Young people in the cities wear jeans and T-shirts.

▲ *In the cities, Western-style clothing is common.*

◄ *Vietnamese women dressed in traditional clothing*

For special occasions such as festivals, most women wear a traditional two-piece outfit. The top is like a long shirt and is worn with pants. Men wear a similar outfit.

△ *Hats are good protection against the weather in Vietnam.*

Hats are worn throughout Vietnam. Cone-shaped hats are the most common. They protect against the hot sun and heavy rain.

Vietnam Today

Vietnam has struggled to improve the lives of its people. In the mid-1980s, Vietnamese leaders intro-

duced a program called *doi moi*. This program included a number of changes for a stable government and economic growth. More Vietnamese run their own small businesses than ever before.

◄ *This couple owns an electric fan company in Ho Chi Minh City.*

Their success encourages others.

Over the past several years, Vietnam has begun working with other nations around the world. But the country still has much more to do.

Thousands of people visit Vietnam each year. They experience its culture and architecture. Cruise ships sail through the country's waters. Life in Vietnam will continue to improve. This interesting country's future looks bright.

▲ *Tourists on the Mekong River*

Glossary

ancestors—members of a person's family who lived a long time ago

communist—relating to a political system in which property is owned by the government and is supposed to be shared by all

deltas—areas of land shaped like a fan where a river enters the sea

lunar—having to do with the moon

monsoons—very strong winds that bring heavy rain

pagodas—types of decorated temples used for worship

typhoons—violent storms that occur in Asia

Did You Know?

- In Chinese, *Nam* means "south." *Viet* means "all the people living south of China."

- There are only about 300 different last names in Vietnam. The most common is Nguyen.

- Special treats enjoyed on Tet include fried watermelon seeds, sweet diced fruit, and pastries wrapped in banana leaves.

- The *dan bau*, part of Vietnamese tradition, is a unique musical instrument. It has one copper string stretched across a large gourd.

At a Glance

Official name: Socialist Republic of Vietnam

Capital: Hanoi

Official language: Vietnamese

National song: "Doan Quan Viet-Nam Di" ("March to the Front")

Area: 128,066 square miles (331,691 square kilometers)

Highest point: Phan Si Pan at 10,312 feet (3,145 meters)

Lowest point: Sea level along the coast

Population: 81,098,416 (2002 estimate)

Head of government: President

Money: Dong

Important Dates

2000 B.C.	Ancestors of today's Vietnamese live in the Red River delta.
800 B.C.	Dong-son people live in the Red River delta.
250 B.C.	Dong-son people become part of the kingdom of Au Lac.
207 B.C.	The Chinese take over the Red River delta.
A.D. 39	The Trung sisters lead a successful fight against the Chinese.
42	The Chinese invade again and rule for nearly 900 years.
939	The Vietnamese declare independence from China.
1400s–1500s	European explorers travel to Vietnam.
1880s	France takes control of Vietnam.
1946	France and Vietnam go to war.
1954	War between France and Vietnam ends, and Vietnam is divided into northern and southern nations.
1957	War between North Vietnam and South Vietnam begins.
1965	The U.S. government sends troops to Vietnam.
1973	The last U.S. troops leave Vietnam.
1975	The Vietnam War ends.
1976	The communists make North Vietnam and South Vietnam one country.
1980s	The Vietnamese government begins a program of economic changes.

Want to Know More?

At the Library

Garland, Sherry. *Children of the Dragon: Selected Tales from Vietnam.* New York: Harcourt, 2001.

McKay, Susan. *Vietnam.* Milwaukee: Gareth Stevens, 1997.

O'Connor, Karen. *Vietnam.* Minneapolis: Carolrhoda Books, 1999.

Roop, Peter, and Connie Roop. *Vietnam.* Des Plaines, Ill.: Heinemann Library, 1998.

On the Web

Vietnamese Language Homepage
http://www.public.asu.edu/~ickpl
For basic information about Vietnam and its language, culture, customs, and history

Vietnam Tourism
http://www.vietnamtourism.com
For places to visit in Vietnam

Through the Mail

Embassy of Vietnam in the United States
1233 20th Street, N.W.
Suite 400
Washington, DC 20036
To learn more about Vietnam and plan a trip to the country

On the Road

Asian Art Museum of San Francisco
200 Larkin Street
San Francisco, CA 94102
415/379-8800
To see sculptures and artwork from Vietnam

Index

About the Author

Sarah E. De Capua enjoys writing about other countries. Researching the manuscripts gives her a chance to read many other books about those countries. Reading good books about faraway places can be a way to visit them!

When she is not working as an author and editor of children's books, De Capua enjoys traveling from her home in Colorado to places she has written about as well as to places she may write about in the future.